Focus on History

edited by Ray Mitchell and Geoffrey Middleton

Life in the
Medieval Monastery
Jane Sayers

Longman

The Monastery

This is a photograph of the monastery at DURHAM, taken from an aeroplane.
We are looking towards the north. Can you see

— the cross-shaped church with a huge tower
— the square cloister where the monks spent much of the day
— the chapter house, with a round end, on the east side of the cloister.
  Here the monks met each day and might be punished if they broke the rules.
— the refectory, where the monks ate, on the south side of the cloister.
  The round kitchen is next to it.
— the dormitory on the west side of the cloister. The monks slept here.
— the tiny round building to the south of the kitchen. It stands on a lawn
  and is surrounded by trees. This was the water tower which brought water
  to the monastery. Find where the water came from.

at Durham

The whole of the monastery is like a great school or college. The road leads to a gate in the wall. Through the gate is the courtyard with the lawn and trees. Near the gate were barns and outbuildings and a guest house. Outside the wall a town grew up.

Now pretend that you are in an aeroplane directly over the monastery at Durham. Make a plan of what you would see, and mark the main buildings. Don't forget to put in the points of the compass. The builders of the Middle Ages made plans like this before they began to build. They arranged the buildings in this way because it was most convenient. In this book you will discover why. You will also be able to find out what life was like in a monastery.

The First Monks

Monks had not always lived together in large buildings like those at Durham. The first monks and nuns were hermits who lived alone. They wanted to think about God. They did not care about food or clothes. They wore rags and ate very little. Some of these monks went to lonely places like Scotland and Ireland.

Gradually monks began to think about living together in little groups. They built themselves a church, and a dining room or refectory, where they might meet. But they still had their separate huts or cells. Look carefully at this photograph, and you will be able to see why they are called *beehive* huts.

Each monk had a hut like this, with a door but no windows.

Round the huts was a wall or palisade, so that it was like a village of monks. This picture shows the Great Skellig Monastery in Ireland. With your friends make a model of some beehive huts and a church. Each hut was cone-shaped and had a hole in the roof to let the smoke from the fire out. Remember to put a wall round the buildings and make the scenery very wild.

St Benedict

Sometimes, when the first monks came to live in groups, they had regular hours for worshipping together, for working and for reading. But they did not have to stay in their monasteries until St Benedict wrote his rule or time-table for monks.

Look at this picture of St Benedict and find
— the book in his right hand
— the crozier or crook in his left hand
— the tonsure or hair cut which showed he was a monk
— the halo or nimbus because he was made a saint.

St Benedict began his life as a hermit. But soon he joined a monastery in Italy and became the chief monk or abbot. There in about the year 530 A.D. he wrote a rule for his monks. The rule was written down in a book. That is why St Benedict is holding one. The rule said that from now on monks had to take vows, that is to make solemn promises. They made three promises. They promised

1 to live as poor people
2 to obey the abbot in all matters
3 not to marry.

The rule also said that they were to live together as one family under the abbot or father for the rest of their lives. They were to try their hardest to be holy and to live like Christ. Only the very good ones became saints.

The Threefold Rule

Here is a picture of St Benedict seated
in a chair. He is showing the rule to his
monks. Can you puzzle out some of the
letters? The rule was written in Latin.
Monks spoke and wrote in Latin.

At the top of the picture you can see
a hand, holding a scroll telling the monks
to be obedient to the abbot.

At the bottom a monk is kissing
St Benedict's foot. He is kneeling on
the ground to show that monks were to
be humble.

The rule is sometimes called the threefold
rule because St Benedict divided the
monks' day into three parts:

a working part,

when the monks had certain jobs to do.
What are these monks doing?

a studying part,

when the monks were to read and learn.
How do we know that this monk became a saint?

and

a praying part,

when the monks went
into the choir of their church to sing and pray.

6

Monks' Clothes

You may be interested in more about what the monks wore. Perhaps you will have seen one. There are still monks and nuns who live according to St Benedict's instructions. St Benedict did not want them to look too grand. He wanted them to wear ordinary clothes, and so monks and nuns today wear the clothes that ordinary people would have worn 1400 years ago.

The long garment is called a habit. The habit was dyed black. The monk also had a cloak with a hood, called a cowl, to protect him from rain, snow, and sun. He wore this over his habit. On his feet he wore sandals, though in cold countries like England he sometimes needed boots. St Benedict was not too severe, saying that the clothes were to be warm enough, were to fit and be comfortable, and were not to be too old. The nun had a black woollen habit just like the monk's, and a white collar called a wimple. Over the wimple she wore a black veil. The veil did not cover her face. It was like a head scarf.

Look carefully at the pictures. Pick out the habit, the cowl, the wimple, the veil and the monks' boots. Do you think these are English monks?

The Abbot
and Abbess

The abbot or father of the monastery
could wear a special hat, like a bishop's, on great
feast days. It was called a mitre. He also had a crozier
or shepherd's crook, and a ring. Sometimes he wore gloves.
This is the tomb of Abbot Newbury of Bristol.
Make a drawing of the mitre and the crozier.
The mitre was made of silk and decorated with
coloured patterns and flowers. The crozier was
made of silver with jewels set in it.
Colour your drawings.

The head of a nunnery was called an abbess.
Here she is.

She ruled over her nuns, as the abbot did
over his monks, and she too had a crozier.
There is a picture of another abbess on page 7.

Becoming a Monk

To become a monk was not very easy. Not that you had to be able to read and write yet, or pass tests. But the abbot had to be sure that the new recruit was suited to the life. If he proved himself to be so, the young man was made a novice for a year. He would be put in the care of the novice master who taught him to behave like the rest. After a year the novice was made a monk. He would make his three promises. (Do you remember what they were?) To show that he had done so, his hair would be clipped, as in the picture.

In the picture you will also be able to see two nuns and an abbess. The abbess and nuns have come to see this monk making his promises. When the novice's hair had been cut, he put on the monk's habit. This ceremony was called **clothing**. This is what the monk looked like after the ceremony.

Make a cut out figure of a monk or nun in cardboard. Cut out a habit, and a cowl or a veil from a piece of black cloth or paper. Remember to leave some tabs so that you can fix them on to your monk or nun. The nun will need a wimple cut out from some white paper. Draw in the boots or sandals, and the tonsure.

9

Building the Monastery

The rule was taken by missionary monks to heathen lands. Pope Gregory the Great sent it to England in 597 with a monk called St Augustine. He set up two monasteries in Canterbury where they kept the rule. Other people built monasteries in other places in England. Try to find out where some of them were, and if they were for monks or for nuns.

Here are some builders building a tower.

Study the picture for a minute or two.

What is the tower made of?

Are the builders monks?

How many kinds of tools and pieces of equipment can you name?

Can you see the foreman or man in charge pointing to a workman to bring another stone up the ladder?

Did you notice the pulley bringing up a wooden bucket, the scaffolding on the top floor, and the man with a plumb line who is seeing that the stones are put in straight?

The Patron

Monasteries needed patrons or great men to endow them. To endow them meant to give them money to build a church and buildings. King Edward the Confessor paid for the building of Westminster abbey, and other kings gave the abbey money and gifts. The kings of France gave money and gifts to the abbey of St Denis. Patrons often liked to stay at their abbeys. Here is a picture of the king of France visiting the monastery of St Denis.

Describe how the monks look on receiving such a visitor.

Monasteries also needed patrons to protect them against invaders who came to steal their wealth. In this picture the monks are having to protect themselves.

What are they throwing at the invaders?

What are the soldiers doing?

The Dedication

Monasteries and nunneries were usually dedicated to, or called after, saints. The monastery at Ely was dedicated to St Etheldreda. When the monks talked about their monastery they called it St Etheldreda's. Sometimes the town took its name from the monastery. Now look carefully at this list.

St Albans

Bury St Edmunds

Peterborough

It is a list of the names of three English towns. To whom were their monasteries dedicated?

O felicia oscula Lactentis labiis impressa. cū
inter crebra indicia reptantis inf... q [n]eie
in pace ver... er te fili? inti alludrer... cū
nerus gr patre... di genit... imparet.

IFREℲMATȟIẴS ꞉ PAꞂISIꞂSꞂꞂꞀ·

A Monk called Matthew

The monk at the bottom
of this picture was called
Brother Matthew Paris. He
has also drawn a picture
of himself and put his name
on it in Latin—
MATHIAS PARISIENSIS
—in the bottom right hand
corner. Find his signature.

Matthew Paris was a
monk at St Albans abbey
in Hertfordshire. He loved
news and gossip and he
wrote a history of his own
time. Fortunately for him
many important guests
came to stay at St Albans
on their way to the North.
Otherwise he might not
have had much to write. For
monks were not allowed to
go out of their monasteries
when they felt like it. They
had to obey the rule or
time-table and spend
equal parts of the day
in work, study and prayer.

Matthew's day
was the same as that of
all the other monks who
had taken vows or made
promises.

The Monks' Day

The Dormitory   The monks slept in a large room called a dormitory. Do you remember the dormitory at Durham, and that it was on one side of the cloister? Here is the dormitory at Cleeve abbey in Somerset. The cloister roof and

arches have now gone, but you can see the little stones called corbels which held the rafters. They are just beneath the windows.

How many windows has the dormitory?

Find the day stairs which lead up to it. They were called the day stairs because this was the staircase used by the monks if they had to go up to the dormitory during the day.

Inside the dormitory, the beds were placed between the windows. Each bed had a mattress, made of straw, a blanket, a coverlet and a pillow.

Matthew in Bed

Here is the monk called Matthew Paris in bed. Look carefully at his clothing. Each monk had a set of night clothes which were very similar to those worn in the day.

Is there a blanket on his bed?

The monks had from six to eight hours' sleep and an afternoon nap in summer. At 2.30 a.m., while it was still dark, the monks were called from their beds for the night service. The monk who woke the others used a time clock.

The Night Stairs

The monks took their lamps and went down the night stairs into the church. Can you see how the monk carried his lantern and how he kept it alight?

The Night Stairs at Hexham

At the top of the stairs is the dormitory door, at the bottom, part of the church called the transept. After the night service the monks went back to bed. At daybreak they were awakened for **Prime**, which was the first service after the sun had risen.

15

16

The Church

The monks spent about a third of the day in church. Do you remember what they did in the other two parts, and why the rule was called the threefold rule? The monks went to the part of the church known as the choir for their services. They sang what is called plain chant.

The choir of the monastery at Canterbury, which you can see opposite, was built by a Frenchman called William of Sens. William of Sens, however, fell from the scaffolding before the choir was finished. He hurt his back and returned home to France. The monks then appointed William the Englishman to finish it.

Here is a list of times when the monks were in church, and the names of their services.

3 a.m.	Night service
6 a.m.	Prime
8 a.m.	Terce
12 noon	Mass
4 p.m.	Vespers
6 p.m.	Compline

A Feast Day or Special Occasion

Everything in the choir was beautiful, especially on important occasions.
Here the monks worshipped God. On special occasions, as when a new
church was dedicated, many people came to see, and sometimes abbots from
other monasteries came too. The abbots wore their mitres and put on
embroidered vestments, and used their best croziers, made of silver or ivory
and studded with jewels. Many candles were lit. Sometimes these had been
painted in gold and colours, like the one at the side of this page.

How many abbots are there in the picture below, and how many monks?
Can you see the people who have come to watch? Two or three
of them are pointing.

There are candles behind the monks' heads as well as on the altar. Also
on the altar you can see a cup or chalice, two candlesticks and a decorated
cloth. In front of the altar is a fine carpet.
Write down why you think this is a great
occasion and feast day.

18

The Cloister

When the service called Prime was over, the monks came out of the church through a door into the cloister. The cloister was the centre of the monastery. Many rooms led off it.

Make a plan of a cloister in your notebook. Leave plenty of space round the cloister so that you can draw other rooms in later. Show the door from the church.

Along one side of the cloister there were studies. The studies were not separate rooms. They were like cubby holes. Each monk or nun had a study. Mark the studies on your plan.

When the monks joined the monastery they had to be taught to read. Some did not find it very easy. Reading and studying took place in the cloister.

The Warming House

Usually the cloister was built on
the south side of the church.
Can you guess why? When the sun
was shining it would be warm in
the cloister. But in the winter,
sitting reading in the cloister,
the monk could get very cold.
The warming house led off
the cloister. Here there was a big
fire-place with a wood fire and
the monks might warm themselves.

Washing

Before they went into the chapter house the monks were allowed to wash. The water was brought into the monastery by lead pipes to a water tower, like the one at Durham on page 2. From the water tower it was fed to the cloister and the kitchen. Water for washing was poured into a long trough or basin in the cloister.

This picture shows the **lavatorium** or washing place at Gloucester. Look closely and you will see how the water drained away.

Opposite the washing trough was an alcove. In it there was a wooden towel cupboard 'kept always with sweet and clean towels' for the monks to dry their hands. This picture shows the alcove. The cupboard has now gone. The monks were told 'not to blow their noses on the towels and not to remove dirt with them'.

You can now put the washing trough and towel cupboard on your plan of the cloister.

The Chapter House

Leading off the cloister was another important room called the chapter house. Put this on your plan. In the chapter house a 'chapter' of the rule was read each day. After that the monks who had not kept the rules were punished. This photograph shows the chapter house at Westminster. It is octagonal in shape. In other words it has eight sides. You can see four of the sides.

Find — the abbot's seat in the centre opposite the entrance

— the monks' stone seats round the walls.

The reader's desk was put in the middle.

This picture is also of the chapter house at Westminster but it is not exactly the same as the photograph on the opposite page. It was drawn in the sixteenth century. Perhaps the artist drew from memory. The floor, however, is the same. Can you see that it is made of tiles? Here are some of the patterns on them.

Make a lino cut or a potato cut of a fish or two lions. You can then print them many times.

Work

There was much work to do in the monastery. After Chapter the monks worked for two hours. Each monk had a task given to him—to work in the kitchen, to help in the guest house, or to look after the poor or sick perhaps. He did this for a week. After that he might be given something else to do. There was a monk in charge of each department. He did not change his job.

The Hospital or Infirmary

When the monks were ill they were taken to the monastery's own hospital or infirmary. The infirmary had its own chapel and kitchen. There was a fire in the infirmary hall and the monks were allowed to eat special food and meat. They were not allowed to eat meat when they were well. At Westminster, the infirmary had a little cloister where the monks could walk and sit and convalesce or get better.

The monk in charge of the infirmary was called the **infirmarian**. Here he is.

He had other monks to help him nurse the sick and old monks. In your book write a sentence about the infirmarian and what he had to do. You will be able to write sentences about other monks and what jobs they did in the monastery when you have learnt about them later on in this book.

The Almonry

St Benedict had said that the monks were to feed, clothe, and look after poor people, as Christ had done. The monk in charge of doing this was called the **almoner**. The almonry building, where the poor were received, was usually near to the wall around the monastery. In this way the monks were not disturbed. This is the almonry at Evesham. Find the gate, through which the poor people entered the monastery, and the abbey wall, which shut the monastery off from the world.

Poor pilgrims, beggars, and disabled people, came to the almonry. You can see them arriving in this picture. Pick out the man with crutches and a bandaged foot, and the pilgrim in a large hat.

The almoner collected what was left over from the monks' meals to give to the poor. He also gave them old clothing. On Thursdays the almoner and his assistants washed poor men's feet. Do you know why?

The Guest House

Travellers often came to stay at monasteries. At an inn the traveller paid for his food and lodging, but at a monastery it was free. The monks had special guest houses, like this one at Dover. The monk in charge of the guest house was called the **hosteller**. (Look up hostel in your dictionary and you will see why.)

Here he is receiving some guests. The hosteller had to see that the guests had clean and untorn towels and sheets, unchipped cups, mattresses, blankets, quilts 'of a pleasing colour', a fire that did not smoke, writing materials, and in winter, candles and candlesticks. He was also to see that the whole guest house was clear of spiders' webs and dirt. The hosteller's servant was not to go to bed until all the guests had retired. He was to be up early to see that the guests did not forget to take their belongings. He was also to see that they did not steal and pack up the monastery's tablecloths, napkins and sheets!

Most guests left the monks a present as they did not have to pay a bill. Some of the rich guests were very mean. King John and all his court stayed at the monastery at Bury St Edmunds for ten days. He left only 13 pence and a silk cloth for which he had not paid.

Write a paragraph about spending a night in the monastery guest house. Remember to say what gift you made to the monks.

The Treasure

Many monasteries were wealthy. They had treasure of gold, silver, and jewels.
People said in the Middle Ages: 'If the abbot of Glastonbury married
the abbess of Shaftesbury, they would be richer than the king of England'.
Of course the rule did not allow them to marry. Monasteries were not
supposed to possess treasure either, but they did, because people gave them
beautiful things, like this golden box
studded with jewels, pearls, rubies,
sapphires and emeralds. In it they might
keep a piece of a garment worn by a saint,
or something which had belonged to the
saint. They also had expensive vessels for
their services, made of gold and silver,
like this silver cup or chalice and this
incense burner.

Find where the incense burner opens, and
where the chain goes through the top.
Look at page 18 and you will see an incense
burner in use.

The Watching Chamber and Guard Duty

Costly ornaments and treasure were not buried, but they were locked away. When they were put on show they were carefully guarded.

This picture shows the watching chamber at St Albans abbey. A monk sat up here to watch for burglars. Some of the treasure was shown in the cupboards beneath, behind a locked grille and locked wooden doors. The doors were opened when people came to see the saint's tomb.

This monk is guarding the tomb of a saint. Do you think he is doing his job well? People often came on pilgrimages to see if the saint could cure them. One of the people kneeling by the tomb has been cured. How do we know this? If you look closely you will see his bandages on the floor. They look rather like snakes. Sometimes people who were cured gave gifts to the monks. The monk in charge of guard duty was called the **sacrist**. He and his assistants kept a watch both night and day.

The Chamberlain

The **chamberlain** looked after the monks' bedding, clothes, and washing and shaving. He had to provide clean straw for the mattresses on the monks' beds once a year, and to see that the covers were kept clean and repaired. He also dealt with the tailors who made the monks their clothes or habits, and he supervised the laundry.

Here he is talking to some of his helpers.

The chamberlain and his staff kept the washing place in the cloister clean and tidy. The monks washed and shaved their own beards daily with their own knives. Every three weeks they had their heads shaved to keep their tonsures in trim. For this the chamberlain had to provide clean towels and hot water. The barber shaved the older monks first. The young monks came last when the water was cold and the towels were wet.

Have you remembered to write sentences about the almoner, the hosteller and the sacrist? Now you can write one about the chamberlain.

The Precentor and Writing

There was much writing to do in the monastery. The precentor had charge of this. Monks wrote charters or letters for the monastery, letters asking people to do things, and letters granting favours. When the letter was written the monk did not sign his name. He put a seal on it. The seal was made of wax.

Look and see how the seal was attached to the letter. The seal was made of bees' wax. When the wax was hot a metal imprint was pressed on it. It made a picture. Perhaps you use sealing wax when you send a parcel. Even today some schools and colleges have imprints to press on wax.

Some monks copied out books by hand. Because there were no printing presses, this was the only way of making more copies.

This monk's name is Eadwine. He made a very beautiful copy of the book of Psalms. He drew this picture of himself on the front page.

Note his desk
      his clean, new book, made of parchment
      his pen
      his knife to rule the lines.

What does the decoration on his chair remind you of?

The School

Monks took boys into the monastery and educated them.
What is happening
in this picture?
Write a paragraph
to describe it.
What is the man
on the left
giving to the monk?

Rich fathers had to pay for their sons' schooling. The boys sang services
with the monks. They had a master in charge of them who taught them, and
who might slap their heads and pull their hair if they were disobedient.

   Poor boys were taken care of in the almonry. They had lessons too, but
not with the rich boys. On feast days there was no school, but the boys
were not allowed to play. They had to repeat by heart their letters and
explain the meaning of words. If they were naughty,
the almoner turned them out of the school and found better behaved ones.
He could also beat them with a rod.

Fields and Lands

St Benedict had said that monks could
worship God by working
in the fields.

What are
these monks
doing?

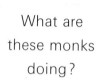

Noblemen gave monasteries gifts of land.
Monks grew corn, owned sheep, mills, and
cattle. They fed themselves from this and
sold the rest.

Some monasteries owned much land and many
villages. Perhaps you live in or near a town
or village called
Abbot's Barton
Abbotsbury
Abbots
Abbots Langley
Newton Abbot
Monkton
Monkland
Hurstbourne Priors
Swaffham Prior
(Prior is just another name for abbot.)
If so, it belonged to a monastery once. Try
to find more examples, and write them down.

Barns

If you look closely you will see that this building has no windows but two huge doors. These were for the carts which brought hay or corn to be stored in this barn.

The barn belonged to the nuns of Shaftesbury. It is at Bradford on Avon. Look on a map of the south of England or in the A.A. book, and find out how far Shaftesbury in Dorset is from Bradford on Avon in Wiltshire. Bradford on Avon is quite a long way to the north of Shaftesbury.

The picture beneath shows what the barn is like inside.

The Bakehouse and the Brewhouse

The monks had servants to bake their bread and brew their ale. For baking and brewing separate buildings were needed. This building was once a brewhouse. Now it is a house. The **cellarer** was in charge of the bakehouse and the brewhouse. He was the most important officer in the monastery after the abbot or prior. He had charge of all the food and drink of the monastery and of the accounts. At Bury St Edmunds, Abbot Sampson gave the **cellarer** a clerk to help him with his sums. A good cellarer did not allow debts.

This is Adam, cellarer of the monastery of St Albans. Can you guess why he carries two huge keys, and what is probably in his bag?

The Kitchen

The **kitchener** worked under the cellarer. He ruled over the kitchen. He had to order all the food and see that the cooking pots were cleaned every day. He also had to see that the food was not stale or badly cooked.

Monks ate one main meal a day, and a lot of fish.
Meat was only eaten by monks who were in the infirmary.

These are some of the things the kitchener ordered: coddes, herring, whitynge, minnows, congers, hallybutt, muscelles, cockylles, mullettes, salt herrings, eeles, carpps, pullets, eggs, cheese, and vegetables'.

He also ordered salt and spices. Monks drank beer, and, on very special occasions, wine.

Pretend you are the kitchener and make a list of the food you need for a week. There are thirty monks in your monastery.

The Refectory

From the kitchen there was a hatch into the refectory. In the refectory the monks ate. They had one main meal a day at 2 o'clock. This was their first big meal, so you can imagine how hungry they were and how they grumbled if their meal was late.

The abbot or prior and his guests sat at the east end of the hall on a raised platform or dais. The monks sat in the main part of the hall at long tables. They were not allowed to talk. Each week a monk was appointed to read during meals. He read the story of a saint's life or perhaps a book which a saint had written. Can you see where the reader stood and how he got up there?

If the monks had nuts to eat, they were not
to crack them with their teeth, but to open
them quietly with their knives. Each monk
had a spoon, his own knife, and a cup. He was
to be careful not to cut the tablecloth with
his knife, not to spill things, and to sit up
properly.

Take a few minutes to study this picture of
a monk eating. Have you noticed
the trestle table
the clean table cloth
the chicken on his plate
the knife in his hand
his bread
his cup?

The Parlour and Recreation

After dinner the monks came out of the refectory into the cloister. Some of them now went to the parlour where they were allowed to talk. The name parlour comes from a French word meaning to talk.

These nuns are talking in their parlour.

And these monks are having a conversation. Monks often sat with their hands in prayer when they were talking. Imagine what they are saying to one another, and write three sentences, one for each.

The younger monks went to play bowls and skittles and other games. You can guess what this nun is playing, and this monk.

The older ones could walk in the garden or play chess, if they did not want to talk or read.

The Library

Some of the monks enjoyed reading after they had had their dinner. Rich monasteries had libraries like this one. Smaller monasteries might have only a cupboard or recess in the cloister to keep books in.

At St Albans abbey, Abbot Simon had his own chest for books.

Here he is looking at one. How do we know that he is the abbot? The picture also shows that books were very precious. If you look very carefully you will see why. Find the parchment roll in the right hand corner of the chest.

Painting

Some monks were good at painting and modelling. They might do this after dinner. This monk is painting a statue.

Do you think he is doing it carefully? Look closely and you will see that he has more than one brush and more than one paint pot. You could make a model in clay of a monk or a nun talking, painting, or playing a game.

The bell rang for Vespers at 4 o'clock. After Vespers came supper and then the last service of the day, Compline. At 6.30 p.m. the monks went to bed. They walked in procession from the cloister to the dormitory, the older and more important monks leading. They got into bed in silence. Their only belongings were a knife, a pen, and a needle. Every day was the same, except in the summer they got up earlier, went to bed later, and had a nap in the afternoon.

Here is their Winter time-table.

2.30 a.m.	Rise	12 noon	Mass
3 a.m.	Night Service	2 p.m.	Dinner
6 a.m.	Prime	3 p.m.	Recreation
7 a.m.	Study	4 p.m.	Vespers
8 a.m.	Chapter and Terce	5.30	Supper
9 a.m.	Work	6 p.m.	Compline
		6.30	Bed

Write a story about a day in a monastery. Give your monk or nun a name, and say what work he or she did.

The Gate

This is the gateway into the monastery of Christ Church, Canterbury. Once the monk had taken his vows he could not go out of the gateway without permission from the abbot.

What has taken the place of a wall on either side of the gate?

Through the gateway you can see part of the church. At the top right, part of the spire.

How many rooms are there over the gateway for the porters? Can you pick out the staircases? They have tiny windows. The small gate was for people on foot. The large gate was opened to let in those on horseback or in carts.

In the centre of the gateway there was once a statue. Each monastery had its own badge or coat of arms. The coat of arms of Christ Church is over the small gate. Make a copy of it in your notebook.

First draw a shield shape.

Then put in a white cross. Colour the background blue. In the middle of the white cross put $\frac{i}{x}$ It should look like this.

Inside the Gateway

At night, when the gates were shut, it looked
like this from the inside. Notice the patterns
on the gates, and the tiny door in the small gate.
All the monks were now in bed, except for those
guarding the treasure. The monks will get up
tomorrow when everybody else is still fast asleep.
They will spend the day in just the same way as
they did yesterday. The rule or time-table had to
be kept every day, every year.

The Abbot's House

The abbot or prior was chosen by the monks as their leader. He did not share their dormitory or refectory. He had his own house, kitchen, dining room, bedrooms, and chapel. Important guests stayed with him and ate at his table, but sometimes he took them to eat in the monks' refectory.

This is the prior's house at Castle Acre monastery in Norfolk.
Look carefully at the picture.
Did you notice the great bay window with the diamond shaped window panes
the oriel window at the end of the house
the doorway
the square windows of the prior's chapel over the doorway
that the house is built joining the church?

Try to find out where else there are abbot's or prior's houses, and if there is one near you.

Here is the inside of the room with the great bay window. The window faced towards the gateway so the abbot could see who came in and who went out. The room was once gay with painting. There were beams across the ceiling like the one above the fireplace. They had red roses painted on them. This room was called the **solar** Now turn over the page and you will see what it looked like when it was lived in.

The Abbot's 'Solar'

Then there would have been
a fire in the hearth
a four poster bed
chairs
a **prie dieu** or desk for
the abbot or prior when he
wished to pray.

What else can you see in
the picture?

Did you notice
the candlestick above
　　　　the fireplace
the apples on the chest
the picture over the abbot's bed
the books on the shelf
the fire tongs
the little dog at the abbot's
feet?

This abbot came from a very
wealthy family, so he could
afford to have his portrait
painted. His name was
Christian de Hondt. Now paint
a portrait of an abbot in his
house. Remember that the
cushions and bed hangings were
made of bright velvet and silks.

The Closing Down of the Monasteries

Look at this picture for a moment. This is Furness abbey in Lancashire as
it is today—a ruin.

When Henry VIII became king of England, he decided that the monasteries
and nunneries had become too wealthy. So he closed them down. The abbots
and monks were given pensions or payments. Some were allowed to become
parish priests. The rich lands of the abbeys were given to King Henry's
friends, and to his important civil servants who had served him well.
The monastery buildings were left to fall down and decay. Sometimes
the church was used as a parish church; then only the other buildings were
left to fall. Sometimes the new owners used the stones to build themselves
houses; sometimes they took over the abbot's house and lived in that.

At Furness abbey, a house was built from the fallen stones. Can you see it on the right of the picture? It has a very neat garden in front. The monastery was used as a park. People went for walks nearby with their dogs. Some rode their horses. Trees grew up among the ruins. Look at the picture carefully and you will see them. Today Furness abbey belongs to the state, and anyone can visit it and try to imagine what it was like when monks lived there.

Some monasteries, like Durham, were also cathedrals or chief churches

of the area. These now had a dean and canons, who were clergymen, but they were not monks living according to a rule. They took over the monastery buildings and made them into houses. If you visit Durham, Canterbury, Ely, Worcester, Chester, or Westminster, and some other places, you will find canons living nowadays in the old monastery buildings.

Draw a map of your area, and mark on it as many monasteries as you can find. Find out if any of them are cathedrals. Mark those you have visited in red.

Index

grandir